Meet Georgia

Illustrated by Marina Muun

Tate Publishing

Georgia O'Keeffe was very good at looking. It might not sound so special, but it was part of what made her an incredible artist. She saw things other people didn't see and found ways to express her feelings through images.

O'Keeffe lived in America in the early twentieth century at a time when society was rapidly changing. Electricity, motor cars, equal rights for women and abstract art were all new. The world was buzzing with new ways of doing things and new ideas.

Being naturally curious, O'Keeffe travelled a lot. She spent time living in different places, including New York and New Mexico. She created paintings and drawings that showed people a unique way of looking at the world.

Come and meet Georgia O'Keeffe! Through her artworks you might find an idea or a way of thinking that is different from yours. You may even find a new way to express your own experiences through art.

In the 1930s, Georgia O'Keeffe lived in two places.

She spent the winter living in New York City and the summer living in the desert in New Mexico.

In New York, tall buildings called 'skyscrapers' blocked out her view of the sky.

In New Mexico, O'Keeffe was surrounded by sky, mountains and dry plains. Sometimes, she slept on the roof to enjoy the view of the sky.

Draw the sky above your house. Can you see it from your bedroom window, or do you have to go outside or onto the roof for a better view?

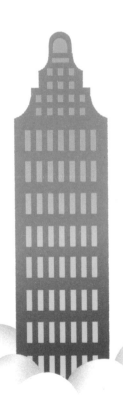

Fill the page with New York skyscrapers.

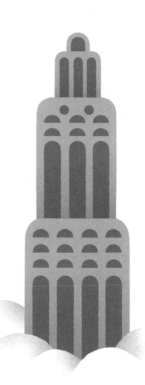

What room, if any, will you leave for the sky?

When she was in New Mexico, Georgia O'Keeffe enjoyed going for long walks and camping in the desert, no matter what the weather!

The Black Place was an area she discovered 150 miles from her house at Ghost Ranch. From a distance, she described it as looking like 'a mile of elephants'.

Imagine you're in the desert and the weather has turned stormy.
Fill the page with wind, rain, hail, clouds and lightning.

Find the way from the Black Place, where Georgia and her friends liked to camp, back to her house at Ghost Ranch.

Black Place

Box Canyon

Chimney Rock

Chapel

Ghost Ranch

River

Abiquiu Reservoir

While she was out walking, Georgia O'Keeffe paid attention to the landscape and how it looked in different lights. In the early morning she often saw pink skies and blue mountains.

Paint the sky above this mountain landscape.
Make it as vibrant and colourful as you can.

What do these shapes look like to you?

Transform these shapes into objects, animals, plants or imaginary creatures.

In Georgia O'Keeffe's painting of two red
poppies, she has zoomed in very close
making them much larger than the real thing.

How might they look if you draw the flowers in a vase …

… or growing in a field of poppies?

Roll this book up, like a telescope. Then find something that is familiar to you (your bed, the television, your favourite toy ...) and examine it closely.

Georgia O'Keeffe often put colours together that were very different from one another. One art writer described her colour combinations as 'tart' like sour berries, 'biting', and 'pungent'.

Experiment by putting colours side by side. Find a pairing that looks:

sickly sweet

salty

hot and spicy

bland and tasteless

sweet and sour

Draw a banquet using unusual and exciting colour combinations.

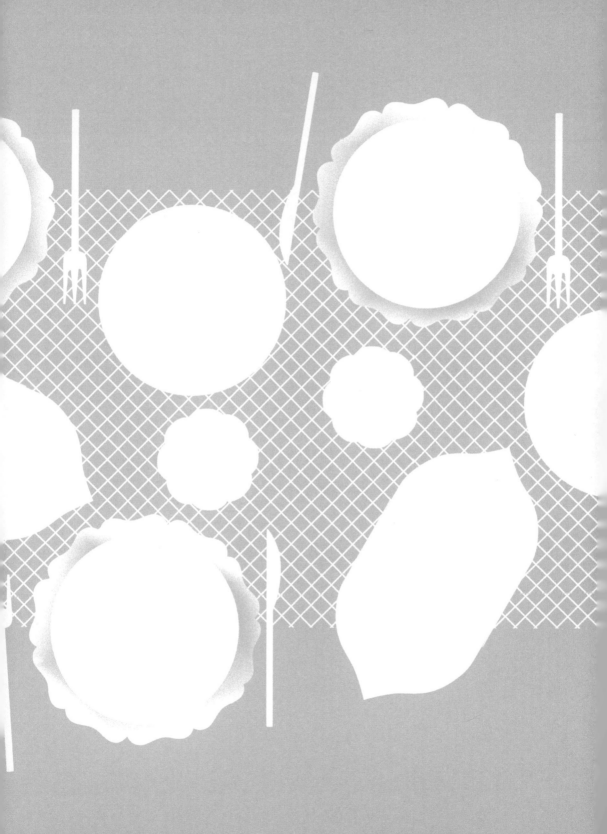

What can you see unfolding in this picture?
Is it a wave, clouds, smoke, a rose or a mountain?

Continue the painting beyond the edges of the image
and show what happens as it continues to unfold.

There were some things Georgia O'Keeffe painted over and over again. One was the door on the side of her house.

Draw your front door six times. Can you make it look different each time?

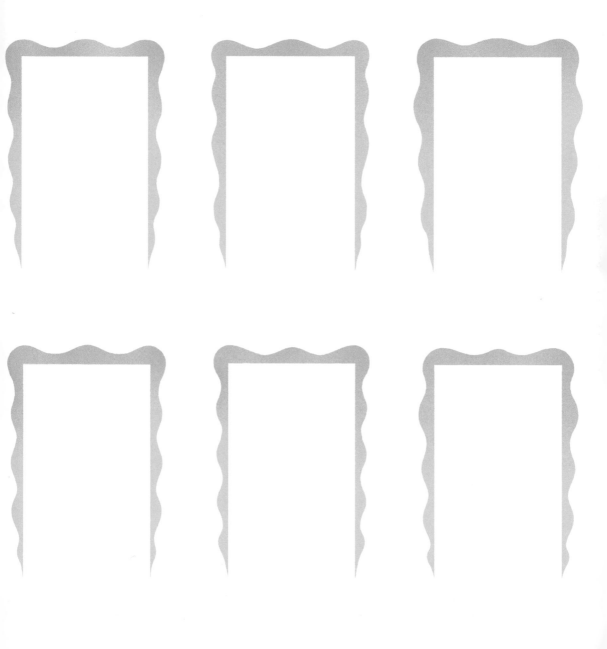

One idea Georgia O'Keeffe explored through her paintings was that music could be expressed through pictures.

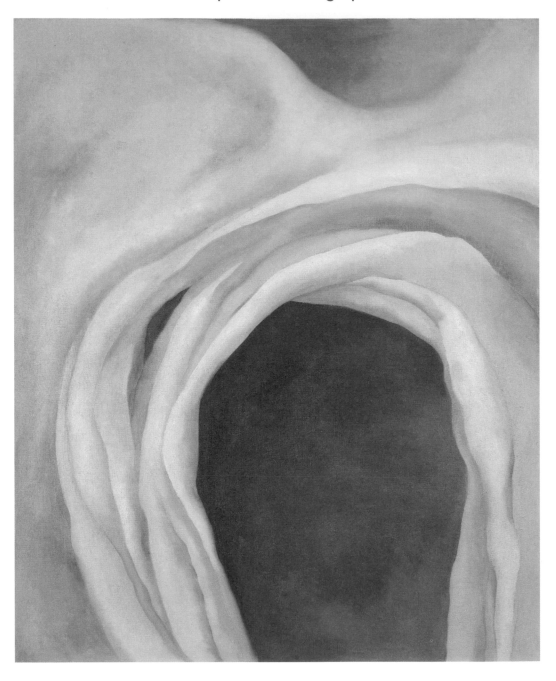

What sort of music do you think Georgia O'Keeffe
was listening to when she created this painting?
Do you think it was an upbeat tune or something soft and gentle?

Choose a song you know well and try drawing it.
Does it sound like wiggly or straight lines?
What colours do each of the instruments sound like?

Experiment with what a fast rhythm might look like and then try a slow one. You can use pencils, crayons or paints to create your song pictures.

This is a drawing of an imaginary song. Can you try humming it?

What happens to your drawing when the rhythm changes?

Paintings by Georgia O'Keeffe

My Backyard 1937
Oil paint on canvas
50.8 x 91.4

New York Street with Moon 1925
Oil paint on canvas
122 x 77

Black Place III 1944
Oil paint on canvas
91.9 x 101.9

Oriental Poppies 1927
Oil paint on canvas
76.2 x 101.6

Abstraction White Rose 1927
Oil paint on canvas
91.4 x 76.2

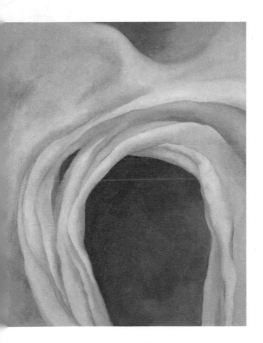

Music - Pink and Blue No. I 1918
Oil paint on canvas
88.9 x 73.7

First published 2016
by order of the Tate Trustees
by Tate Publishing,
a division of Tate Enterprises Ltd,
Millbank, London SW1P 4RG
www.tate.org.uk/publishing

A catalogue record for this book is available from
the British Library
ISBN 978 1 84976 487 2

Distributed in the United States and Canada by
ABRAMS, New York

Library of Congress Control Number applied for

Designed by Nous Vous
Colour reproduction by Evergreen Colour
Management Ltd, Hong Kong
Printed and bound in Spain by Grafos SA

Measurements of artworks are given in
centimetres, height before width

Copyright credits

Page 4:
New York Street with Moon
1925
Oil paint on canvas
122 x 77
Carmen Thyssen-Bornemisza Collection on loan
at the Museo Thyssen-Bornemisza, Madrid

Page 4:
My Backyard
1937
Oil paint on canvas
50.8 x 91.4
The New Orleans Museum of Art: Museum
Purchase, City of New Orleans Capital Funds

Page 8:
Black Place III
1944
Oil paint on canvas
91.9 x 101.9
Georgia O'Keeffe Museum, Gift of The Burnett
Foundation, 2007

Page 16:
Oriental Poppies
1927
Oil paint on canvas
76.2 x 101.6
The Collection of the Frede
Art Museum at the Uni
Minneapolis. Museu

Page 24:
Abstraction White Ro
1927
Oil paint on canvas
91.4 x 76.2
Georgia O'Keeffe Museum, Gift of The Burnett
Foundation and The Georgia O'Keeffe Foundatio

Page 26:
Music – Pink and Blue No. I
1918
Oil paint on canvas
88.9 x 73.7
Collection of Mr and Mrs Barney A. Ebsworth